It's Time to

COWBOY UP

The Demise of the American Male

STAN LAMACKI

"The Logic of English®" sheets at the back of the book are reprinted with permission of Pedia Learning Inc.

"It's Time to Cowboy Up," By Stan Lamacki. ISBN 978-1-62137-964-5 (softcover); 978-1-62137-965-2 (eBook).

Published 2017 by Virtualbookworm.com Publishing Inc., P.O. Box 9949, College Station, TX , 77842, US.

TABLE OF CONTENTS

TABLE OF CONTENTS

INTRODUCTION

Caveats

SINCE THE LATE 1960s, America has seen the decline in the overall status of men. In recent times, this decline has become more pronounced. One of the most obvious indications comes from the U.S. Census Bureau, which reveals that women currently make up 54% of the U.S. work force. The income of the American male continually declines, unemployment of the American male continues to increase, and jobs males typically would hold (manufacturing, industrial production, business and logistics) are constantly disappearing; either going to other countries or planned obsolescence.

Today, too many American men are unemployed, broke, dependent, uneducated, and weakened by forces they may not recognize as causing their demise. Pressure from economic and social forces put the future of the American male in jeopardy. Of course, lack of initiative, criminality, laziness, and stupidity are additional liabilities to their plight.

So, why the cowboy? Because the image is rugged, open, strong, indedpendent, self-directed, forthright, stoic, and self-assured. The cowboy also takes care of himself and his own; qualities that moved the American male to past economic success and prominence. The cowboy image is one that can be easily related to — it represents a style and way of living the American male can aspire to while turning around his current negative circumstances. This is not, however, a plea to return to the "golden days of yesteryear."

The cowboy went to where the work was — Texas, Oklahoma, Colorado. When work got scarce, they moved to other places: New Mexico, Arizona, California, Wyoming, Montana. They learned how to do something else, usually out of survival and pride. Today, with the scarcity of "old school" jobs, the American male needs to wake up to these facts.

Big manufacturing is gone. The steel industry is not coming back; the U.S. government refused to subsidize or bail it out. Although they bailed out Chrysler, General Motors (twice), the financial industry, etc. Big machinery has moved to Mexico and overseas because the U.S. government refused to give them tax breaks and other concessions. Coal mining is gone due to a myriad of suffocating government regulations. All of this caused the loss of millions of decent-paying jobs the American male would generally fill. Currently, in many cities, there are good jobs going unfilled, such as tradesmen, electricians, carpenters, brick layers, HVAC installers, and auto mechanics. There are other industries with openings, such as truck drivers and health care workers. Solar panel and wind turbine companies are also looking for help in the manufacturing side.

There are jobs out there for the American male, but to get one, he must "cowboy up" and get training in those fields and be willing to move to where they are, just as the real cowboys did. There is training out there for those fields, some at a cost and some for free. Job training programs are offered by states, cities, municipalities, counties, and even trade unions. There are legitimate, for-profit schools that offer training. There are also regular community and four-year colleges seeking students. If money is an issue, don't be afraid of loans. Training is key. Even someone had to teach cowboys how to ride, rope, and herd. So get up off your butt and COWBOY UP.

There are some caveats, stipulations, admonitions, and warnings the cowboys of today must understand. The primary one is that the American male is any male (GBTQ)citizen, visa, green card holder, or illegal alien who earns money in the U.S. in any form or is unemployed or totally broke. It doesn't matter where the money comes from. The American male is of any race or religion; he could be White, Asian, Black, Hispanic, Native American, Mid-Eastern, Buddhist, Christian, Islamic, Shinto, Hindu, agnostic, Jewish, atheist, it does not matter.

Also, there should be no discrimination regarding employment, housing, buying and selling, or in any other scenario. Since money is issued by the U.S. Government, then it must be accepted anywhere, anytime, for any reason by anyone and everyone. The American male cowboy has one color – FEDERAL GREEN. If you cannot accept all of this, GET OFF THE RANCH.

The Set Up

Since 2008, the United States economy for the American male has been a roller coaster ride, with each final landing trending downward. Whether it has been higher unemployment, lower stock market prices, lack of decent-paying jobs, poor or slow consumer spending, or pressure from foreign markets and banks, our national economy and outlook have generally decreased. Some of these factors can be affected by government policies and some resist any government intervention. Government at every level — federal, state, county, city, municipal — are decrying the lack of tax revenue needed to fund their programs. Working people bemoan their own lack of sufficient income to provide for their families and themselves, and save for the future. The poor wonder what happened to the safety net which provides for their basic needs. To those Americans who would criticize this group, take a look around and see the increasing number of hungry and homeless in this country. At the national and personal levels, America and Americans are BROKE-ASS. This economic downturn has affected almost 85% of Americans. It has most strongly affected the male population, regardless of race, and for them the recovery has been slow, unfulfilling, and will never be complete.

Yes, the federal government is as broke ass as the American male. Look at the federal deficit and the national debt. Many states and cities cannot service their debt, have to cut back on services, have not paid into obligated pension programs, have borrowed from banks, have issued bonds and funds which they cannot service, financial rating companies have lowered their status to junk, and one major city, Detroit, went into bankruptcy. The Detroit bankruptcy affected all but the top 5% of income earners. The phony rebuilding program there may cause another financial disaster, and now other cities are mulling over the possibility of bankruptcy.

And it's not just governments, it's businesses and individuals as well. Companies and small business are filing for bankruptcy or reorganization at alarming rates. Companies are closing stores, branches, and locations, laying off thousands of people monthly. The economic news continues to be negative. Those who have lost a job, high-paying or not, are unable to find work with similar pay and benefits and are forced to take lower-paying, non-benefit jobs, or no employment at all, becoming dependent on unemployment benefits which eventually run out.

Individuals and families overspend and over-extend credit, thinking tomorrow will be better. When tomorrow doesn't come, they reach out to that TV lawyer promising relief and salvation (FOR A SWEET FEE!). The fight for $15 per hour seems useless when you were making $60 per hour. College for you and your children – GONE! Yes, we are a BROKE-ASS nation.

Don't be misled by government unemployment figures. At the time of writing, the current claim is that the rate is at 4.8%. This number does not include those who have stopped looking for work, those with part-time employment, and those who have never been in the labor force; there are more of these people than you think. The real unemployment rate is closer to 18.5%. With the estimated U.S population of 324 million and those eligible for work at 220 million adults — and using the government's figure of 2.4% unemployment as being considered full employment, — there should be 214 million adults in the labor force. The current labor force is about 170 million, therefore 44 million people are out of work, or 18.5%. So, only 52% of the population is working. If you're one of the unemployed, it's time to COWBOY UP.

Most economists, and the federal government, consider that 67% to 75% of the U.S economy depends on consumer spending. If the country had 214 million full-time workers spending their pay, this economy would be moving faster than the bean counters could add. Unfortunately, this government does not support job creation in real industries such as mining, manufacturing, building, and product development. Instead it supports green, robotic, pharmaceutical, soft services, and other non-production tech industries; all of which cause job loss, underpaid entry jobs, shrinking part-time employment, and other types of unemployment. A business maxim that has produced jobs and money for thousands of years is "wealth comes from the earth."

Between 1950 and now, America has had 13 presidents. Some were liked, some were not. Some served for the maximum two terms and some were fill-ins or began that way. During the time span these presidents served, there has been an assassination, an attempted assassination, a resignation, an attempted coup by a military general, and an impeachment proceeding. Despite this, the nation still stands, the government operates, and the union remains intact. No matter what turmoil or dissent a presidential election might create, the branches of government continue to function. Through all the good, bad, great, terrible and in-between times in America, all continues on in our democracy. The Constitution still stands.

Observations & Thoughts

It has been a pleasure to teach at all levels — elementary, high school, and college (more in chapter 6). It has been an even greater pleasure to tour 36% of the states and numerous cities and towns. Throughout these travels, there have been countless encounters and observations of people from all demographics (race, sex, age, etc.) and income levels — from stone-broke, homeless to millionaires and their stylish cars. People ranging from totally negative to completely positive attitudes, different lifestyles, and various dreams and aspirations have been viewed. Most of those encountered are not doing well socially and, most importantly, economically – especially the American male. It is this group that is being addressed and in which these observations and thoughts are presented.

As with all observations, codifications and research should be validated by the author's point of view, hypotheses, references, philosophical outlook, and biases. To this end, the following disclaimers are posited:

If you are college educated, you probably don't need to read this.

If you can read at the 12th grade level, you will not need any assistance in reading this.

The American male as defined here is any male who lives in the United States and transacts any business with American money regardless of citizenship, alien status (legal or illegal), race, creed, color, ethnicity, ancestry, national origin, heritage, or sexual orientation.

The LGBTQ community is entitled to and deserve all rights as afforded in the U.S. Constitution without discrimination or harassment.

Mark Twain wrote, "There are lies, damned lies, and statistics." Any research and/or numbers provided here are from the federal government, Census Bureau, GSA, IRS, and financial companies. Often, an average is presented.

"The first rule of government is to ensure civil obedience," - George Will. With this in mind, beware any government, as they will always protect themselves.

"Absolute power corrupts absolutely." – John Dalberg-Acton. Take a look around and see if that isn't true.

"That government which governs least, governs best." – Henry David Thoreau. Good luck with that.

"Question everything, learn something, answer nothing." – Euripides. A great day-to-day code of living and learning.

With the above statements in mind, the following observations and thoughts are presented in the spirit and desire to improve the condition of the American male. Agreement or disagreement will occur, along with some serious thought, laughter, and anger.

If the main purpose of government, as George Will reasons, is to ensure domestic obedience, the easiest way to ensure this is to keep people broke. If you trust that any form of government acts in your best interest, economically and socially, then you must be independently wealthy. Government actions generally disenfranchise or marginalize those who do not have enough money to live on or who are struggling to save and invest in order to have a better future. The graduated and dual tax systems for individuals and corporations put the heaviest burden on individuals and married couples whose household incomes range from $50,000 to $240,000 annually. They are taxed at an inordinate rate and have limited deductions. At a different level, but just as appalling, look at the incredibly high fees of operating an automobile — plates, stickers, parking fees, gasoline taxes. Sales, property, liquor, water, garbage, sewer, and other municipal taxes keep money out of your hands. This ensures the government will keep you compliant and obedient because you are too broke to do anything. If you don't think this is true, check your wallet.

Aside from power, the government understands only two things and fears them both. They are MONEY and VOTING. The government is scared of the ballot box. They have numerous devices in place to prevent people from voting. If everyone who could vote and would do so, that would be total anarchy to whoever is in power. Voting gives the individual power; the power to be heard with the possibility for change. If everyone eligible would vote, the two party system would begin to crumble and smaller parties with their candidates would be heard thus challenging the old guard. That would drive the democrats and republicans crazy. They may even have to submit to the voice of the electorate. If you don't vote, you really have nothing to say about government actions affecting your life because you've not made any choice.

The second item the government fears is money and what you do with your money. The government runs on taxes as previously mentioned. They must have tax dollars or a shutdown is eminent.

By the government's own accounting office, the GAO, and independent financial sources, the economy is fueled by consumer spending. Estimates are that this comprises 67-to-72% of economic activity. It follows that this generates up to 35% of all government taxes, which helps keep you poor. Imagine if consumers stopped spending. The government would scream bloody murder. If consumers would slow down or stop their spending, the voice of the electorate would certainly be heard. Don't say economic boycotts don't work. Cesar Chavez changed labor, Dr. Martin Luther King revitalized a nation, Mahatma Ghandi created a country.

The reason any business exists — public, private, or non-profit — is to separate you from your money. Think about any media advertising you hear or see — radio, television, newspapers, magazines, billboards, internet and cell phone banners. No matter what the product, the message is BUY ME, give me your money. That's their sole purpose. Is it really that important to buy that or give to that?

Rampant, uncontrolled, conspicuous consumerism will make you broke. If you spend all the money you have, or more, then you won't have any. The government and economists decry that people don't save enough money for retirement, and at the same time complain when they don't spend because it hurts taxes and the general economy. They talk out of both sides of their mouths. You can't have it both ways.

It's interesting that in certain countries the poor have more and better guns. Terrorists who don't have a permanent home, a regular job, or enough food, militias in poor and third-world countries, impoverished Eastern Europeans, middle east and African tribesmen all have great weapons. They have fully automatic weapons, machine guns, grenade and rocket launchers, IEDs, bombs, mortars, and other devices. Two questions arise. Where and how do they get them, and where are yours, cowboy? If you live in a mostly industrialized country, such as America, China, Japan, France (who supplies most of these items to the mentioned poor), England, Canada, Germany, Spain, etc., you are limited to the type, size, and style of gun you can own — IF AT ALL. You are limited and placed at a disadvantage by your own government. They are limiting your ability to defend your life and property. The government cannot protect you. Look at the destruction of 9/11, terrorist bombings and shootings in America, and just general crime.

Every government decision affects your money whether they result in higher taxes, the price you pay for goods and services, or the reduction in a product to cover increased costs. Some examples include minimum wage hikes, the Affordable Care Act, FDA drug approval, smaller items for the same or more money, and any increased spending for a government program.

You are no more important than anyone else. This also means no one is better than you. Of course, there are some exceptions — those who have their asses wiped by someone else like the Pope, the emperor of Japan, the Aga Kahn, Dali Llama, babies, those in nursing homes, and some disabled folks. If someone else wipes your ass, you are special.

There are always off-the-wall, single thoughts that occur randomly. It does not mean they are not worthy of consideration, it's just that happen randomly. So think about some of the following thoughts.

There is no more effective consumer tool than the economic boycott.

Facebook is possibly the platform for the bored and boring.

Among the reasons for violence in America is that we are a diverse culture and that diversity is not respected.

Everyone, regardless of anything, has the same rights as you.

No one has the right to invade your space unless you want them to.

Those who have money spend less than they take in.

Government, at all levels, is generally and somehow corrupt.

Forty-seven percent of adults Americans cannot immediately come up with $400.00 to cover an emergency.

Identity politics, individualizing the agenda of a small group, is causing more division and derision in our society.

Stuff I don't see, and won't see kids doing anymore:

- Pitching pennies on the sidewalk or against a wall
- Playing mumble peg

- Playing cops & robbers or cowboys and Indians with cap guns
- Playing a pick-up baseball game in the park
- Playing in a sand box
- Playing in a park altogether
- Buying a candy bar at a local drug store
- Buying a comic book at a local drug store
- Going to a local theatre on a holiday to see cartoons
- Returning bottles for cash
- Mowing lawns or shoveling snow for cash
- Having a fist fight to settle differences
- Buying a pretzel stick from a countertop canister
- Playing board games, including chess
- Model railroading or road racing

NO! – They have computers!

Broke-Ass & Dumb-Ass American Men

The state of the American male is weak. Too many are unemployed or underemployed, uneducated or undereducated, in the wrong field, poor, broke, or near broke, losing ground, or just plain lazy or dumb – or all of these. These traits give us the BROKE-ASS and or DUMB-ASS American man.

You know you're a Broke-Ass or Dumb-Ass or both if:

- You spend every penny you get
- You're living off your woman
- Your main source of income comes from stealing
- Your retirement plan is winning the lottery
- You have no savings
- You buy food on a credit card and can't pay the monthly balance
- Your debt, minus mortgage, is more than your savings
- You spend more than you make
- Your cell phone is your most expensive possession
- Your income is from being a drug mule
- You don't have money in your pocket that you don't need
- You beat your woman for any (or no) reason
- You think Jerry, Steve, and Oprah are journalists

- You think that US and People magazines are literature
- Your best dress shoes are Nikes
- You have to hold your pants up when running
- You constantly need and seek the approval of others
- You constantly complain and gripe about your situation
- You're always eating out and buying Starbuck's coffee
- You think reality TV shows are real
- You think TV shows are real and important
- You're more concerned with the opinions of others
- Your underwear is exposed
- Your dress outerwear is a dark-colored hoodie
- You don't speak properly among company
- You have poor table manners and other social skills
- You think non-profit organizations don't make money
- You blame "THEM" for your failures
- You think the government wants to help you
- Math is a secret code you can't break

Cowboy Up

OK, gentlemen, it's time to Cowboy Up. Do what will improve your status and income. You can Cowboy Up and not give in to the white, don't-need-to/want-to-work, female agenda. You know the non-working women and emasculated, stubble-bearded men's groups that gave us PETA; Save the Whales; Greenpeace; ASPCA; Occupy Wall Street; Fight for Fifteen; ban plastic bags/bottles; vegetarianism; paleomania; global warming-ism; cage-free, organic, hormone-free, antibiotic-free (did you ever see what a chicken eats?), gluten-free, fair-trade, whole-foods craze; along with other "isms" and various " I have nothing else to do" movements sapping your manhood. Stop being emasculated by these groups and COWBOY UP.

Following are a few suggestions to help you on your way.

- Follow your own agenda – be your own man.
- Don't worry about political correctness, but be polite. We are all human beings.
- You don't have to agree with anyone's lifestyle, but allow them to have it. They have the same rights as you.
- Get a job; it doesn't matter what.
- If you need, get educated — GED, High School, Trade school, etc.
- It's OK to have your own opinions even if they're not popular.

- It's OK to be a male.
- Dress for the situation; look and act like you're somebody.
- Get off social media and stop giving out your personal information — be mysterious, like the lone cowboy.
- Forget the word fair, unless you are referring to a state or county carnival with corn dogs, elephant ears, the grange building, and 4H tents. There is equity and parity often interrupted by the rule of law.
- If you need to respond to a statement you don't like, let your answer be, "Is that right?"
- Generally, keep your mouth shut.
- If asked anything you don't like, remember that "you don't know nothin' about nothing."
- Don't converse about NASCAR or wrestling with a woman.
- The Civil War ended 0ver 160 years (seven to eight generations) ago; way past time to get over it.
- Grow up and get over yourself. You're not that special, important, or good looking. No one is. One monkey don't stop no show.
- There's a sucker born every minute. Don't be one.

OK, Cowboy, eat that gluten, drink real milk, have ice cream, enjoy chicken, beef, veal, pork, lamb, etc., throw down a handful of peanuts, buy a gas guzzler. It's your money to do with as you please. The only conspiracies are the liberal left wingers and

Madison Avenue advertising executives telling you what to buy, what to believe, and how to feel.

All that may be left to say here is that if you're not willing to Cowboy Up, then get off the range, get off the trail, get out of the barn, get away from the chuck wagon, get out of the bunkhouse, get off the farm, jump off the buckboard, and keep away from the branding iron.

COWBOY UP !!!!!!

Minimum Knowledge

As mentioned earlier, it has been a pleasure and honor to teach at the elementary, high school, and college levels. It is disheartening to discover what too many 18-year-olds don't know or can't do. There are even students at the senior college level who lack certain reading and math skills that would be minimally needed in the employment and market place. These deficiencies often prevent the American male from being able to Cowboy Up and secure adequate employment. Following is a brief summation of certain minimal skills required to have a chance at economic attainment.

Math skills are woefully lacking in many people. Some don't even recognize the symbols, let alone the calculations. Minimally, a person should know how to add (+) column addition, 4 columns of 3 digits each with regrouping (carrying).

```
   365
   796
   421
 + 189
= 1771
```

Subtraction (-) 2 column, 3digit, with regrouping:

```
   541
  -269
  =272
```

Multiplication (x) 3 digit by 2 digit, with carrying

379
x 37
=14203

Division (/) 2 digits into 3 digits with converted remainders

47/523 = 11.12

Multiplication tables up to 12 times should be part of memory.

Concepts as 1st 2nd 3rd are minimum. What are cardinal and ordinal numbers.

Simple word problems that show multiple steps in order to understand sequence are of great benefit.

Basic shapes should be known: square, circle, rectangle, triangle, parallelogram, trapezoid, octagon, oval.

People need to know how to find area and linear measures, and understand and calculate the circumference, diameter, and radius of a circle. Basic measurements of inches, feet, yards, centimeters, meters, kilometers, ounces, pounds, grams, kilograms, the concept of Pi, square root, square and cube root.

In writing, one should know both cursive writing and print. Filling out a job form or just writing a simple thank you note is very important.

In regard to reading, the most successful readers have a sight word vocabulary — words you don't even need to think about because you recognize them just by looking at them — of about 1700 words. This list is included after the required readings.

Some of these things may seem unreasonable to the American male who did not graduate high school, but this knowledge can be acquired without too much difficulty. Every community has free or reduced-price educational courses and help. Places such as the YMCA, community colleges, city and volunteer help centers, and charitable organizations are available to those willing to put in some effort.

So, come on, Cowboy. Take advantage of every available opportunity to better yourself and improve your lot. Be the American Cowboy you're meant to be.

SADDLE UP! LET'S RIDE!

Required Readings

Although there are so many more readings the cowboy should be aware of, attached are four every cowboy should review. Three are the basis of our American freedoms and opportunities and the fourth an insightful column (his last one) written by the journalist Charley Reese.

The Magna Carta

The Rights of Man

The U.S. Constitution

The Charley Reese Column

THE MAGNA CARTA

(The Great Charter)

PREPARED BY Nancy Troutman (The Cleveland Free-Net - aa345). Distributed by the Cybercasting Services Division of the National Public Telecomputing Network (NPTN).

Maintained: Jon Roland of the Constitution Society

John, by the grace of God, king of England, lord of Ireland, duke of Normandy and Aquitaine, and count of Anjou, to the archbishop, bishops, abbots, earls, barons, justiciaries, foresters, sheriffs, stewards, servants, and to all his bailiffs and liege subjects, greetings. Know that, having regard to God and for the salvation of our soul, and those of all our ancestors and heirs, and unto the honor of God and the advancement of his holy Church and for the rectifying of our realm, we have granted as underwritten by advice of our venerable fathers, Stephen, archbishop of Canterbury, primate of all England and cardinal of the holy Roman Church, Henry, archbishop of Dublin, William of London, Peter of Winchester, Jocelyn of Bath and Glastonbury, Hugh of Lincoln, Walter of Worcester, William of Coventry, Benedict of Rochester, bishops; of Master Pandulf, subdeacon and member of the household of our lord the Pope, of brother Aymeric (master of the Knights of the Temple in England), and of the illustrious men William Marshal, earl of Pembroke, William, earl of Salisbury, William, earl of Warenne, William, earl of Arundel, Alan of Galloway (constable of Scotland), Waren Fitz Gerold, Peter Fitz Herbert, Hubert De Burgh (seneschal of Poitou), Hugh de Neville, Matthew Fitz Herbert, Thomas Basset, Alan Basset, Philip d'Aubigny, Robert of

Roppesley, John Marshal, John Fitz Hugh, and others, our liegemen.

1. In the first place we have granted to God, and by this our present charter confirmed for us and our heirs forever that the English Church shall be free, and shall have her rights entire, and her liberties inviolate; and we will that it be thus observed; which is apparent from this that the freedom of elections, which is reckoned most important and very essential to the English Church, we, of our pure and unconstrained will, did grant, and did by our charter confirm and did obtain the ratification of the same from our lord, Pope Innocent III, before the quarrel arose between us and our barons: and this we will observe, and our will is that it be observed in good faith by our heirs forever. We have also granted to all freemen of our kingdom, for us and our heirs forever, all the underwritten liberties, to be had and held by them and their heirs, of us and our heirs forever.

2. If any of our earls or barons, or others holding of us in chief by military service shall have died, and at the time of his death his heir shall be full of age and owe "relief", he shall have his inheritance by the old relief, to wit, the heir or heirs of an earl, for the whole barony of an earl by £100; the heir or heirs of a baron, £100 for a whole barony; the heir or heirs of a knight, 100s, at most, and whoever owes less let him give less, according to the ancient custom of fees.

3. If, however, the heir of any one of the aforesaid has been under age and in wardship, let him have his inheritance without relief and without fine when he comes of age.

4. The guardian of the land of an heir who is thus under age, shall take from the land of the heir nothing but reasonable produce, reasonable customs, and reasonable services, and that without destruction or waste of men or goods; and if we have committed the wardship of the lands of any such minor to the sheriff, or to any other who is responsible to us for its issues, and he has made destruction or waster of what he holds in wardship, we will take of him amends, and the land shall be committed to two lawful and discreet men of that fee, who shall be responsible for the issues to us or to him to whom we shall assign them; and if we have given or sold the wardship of any such land to anyone and he has therein made destruction or waste, he shall lose that wardship, and it shall be transferred to two lawful and discreet men of that fief, who shall be responsible to us in like manner as aforesaid.

5. The guardian, moreover, so long as he has the wardship of the land, shall keep up the houses, parks, fishponds, stanks, mills, and other things pertaining to the land, out of the issues of the same land; and he shall restore to the heir, when he has come to full age, all his land, stocked with ploughs and wainage, according as the season of

husbandry shall require, and the issues of the land can reasonable bear.

6. Heirs shall be married without disparagement, yet so that before the marriage takes place the nearest in blood to that heir shall have notice.

7. A widow, after the death of her husband, shall forthwith and without difficulty have her marriage portion and inheritance; nor shall she give anything for her dower, or for her marriage portion, or for the inheritance which her husband and she held on the day of the death of that husband; and she may remain in the house of her husband for forty days after his death, within which time her dower shall be assigned to her.

8. No widow shall be compelled to marry, so long as she prefers to live without a husband; provided always that she gives security not to marry without our consent, if she holds of us, or without the consent of the lord of whom she holds, if she holds of another.

9. Neither we nor our bailiffs will seize any land or rent for any debt, as long as the chattels of the debtor are sufficient to repay the debt; nor shall the sureties of the debtor be distrained so long as the principal debtor is able to satisfy the debt; and if the principal debtor shall fail to pay the debt, having nothing wherewith to pay it, then the sureties shall answer for the debt; and let them have the lands and rents of the debtor, if they

desire them, until they are indemnified for the debt which they have paid for him, unless the principal debtor can show proof that he is discharged thereof as against the said sureties.

10. If one who has borrowed from the Jews any sum, great or small, die before that loan be repaid, the debt shall not bear interest while the heir is under age, of whomsoever he may hold; and if the debt fall into our hands, we will not take anything except the principal sum contained in the bond.

11. And if anyone die indebted to the Jews, his wife shall have her dower and pay nothing of that debt; and if any children of the deceased are left under age, necessaries shall be provided for them in keeping with the holding of the deceased; and out of the residue the debt shall be paid, reserving, however, service due to feudal lords; in like manner let it be done touching debts due to others than Jews.

12. No scutage not aid shall be imposed on our kingdom, unless by common counsel of our kingdom, except for ransoming our person, for making our eldest son a knight, and for once marrying our eldest daughter; and for these there shall not be levied more than a reasonable aid. In like manner it shall be done concerning aids from the city of London.

13. And the city of London shall have all it ancient liberties and free customs, as well by land as by

water; furthermore, we decree and grant that all other cities, boroughs, towns, and ports shall have all their liberties and free customs.

14. And for obtaining the common counsel of the kingdom anent the assessing of an aid (except in the three cases aforesaid) or of a scutage, we will cause to be summoned the archbishops, bishops, abbots, earls, and greater barons, severally by our letters; and we will moveover cause to be summoned generally, through our sheriffs and bailiffs, and others who hold of us in chief, for a fixed date, namely, after the expiry of at least forty days, and at a fixed place; and in all letters of such summons we will specify the reason of the summons. And when the summons has thus been made, the business shall proceed on the day appointed, according to the counsel of such as are present, although not all who were summoned have come.

15. We will not for the future grant to anyone license to take an aid from his own free tenants, except to ransom his person, to make his eldest son a knight, and once to marry his eldest daughter; and on each of these occasions there shall be levied only a reasonable aid.

16. No one shall be distrained for performance of greater service for a knight's fee, or for any other free tenement, than is due therefrom.

17. Common pleas shall not follow our court, but shall be held in some fixed place.

18. Inquests of novel disseisin, of mort d'ancestor, and of darrein presentment shall not be held elsewhere than in their own county courts, and that in manner following; We, or, if we should be out of the realm, our chief justiciar, will send two justiciaries through every county four times a year, who shall alone with four knights of the county chosen by the county, hold the said assizes in the county court, on the day and in the place of meeting of that court.

19. And if any of the said assizes cannot be taken on the day of the county court, let there remain of the knights and freeholders, who were present at the county court on that day, as many as may be required for the efficient making of judgments, according as the business be more or less.

20. A freeman shall not be amerced for a slight offense, except in accordance with the degree of the offense; and for a grave offense he shall be amerced in accordance with the gravity of the offense, yet saving always his "contentment"; and a merchant in the same way, saving his "merchandise"; and a villein shall be amerced in the same way, saving his "wainage" if they have fallen into our mercy: and none of the aforesaid amercements shall be imposed except by the oath of honest men of the neighborhood.

21. Earls and barons shall not be amerced except through their peers, and only in accordance with the degree of the offense.

22. A clerk shall not be amerced in respect of his lay holding except after the manner of the others aforesaid; further, he shall not be amerced in accordance with the extent of his ecclesiastical benefice.

23. No village or individual shall be compelled to make bridges at river banks, except those who from of old were legally bound to do so.

24. No sheriff, constable, coroners, or others of our bailiffs, shall hold pleas of our Crown.

25. All counties, hundred, wapentakes, and trithings (except our demesne manors) shall remain at the old rents, and without any additional payment.

26. If anyone holding of us a lay fief shall die, and our sheriff or bailiff shall exhibit our letters patent of summons for a debt which the deceased owed us, it shall be lawful for our sheriff or bailiff to attach and enroll the chattels of the deceased, found upon the lay fief, to the value of that debt, at the sight of law worthy men, provided always that nothing whatever be thence removed until the debt which is evident shall be fully paid to us; and the residue shall be left to the executors to fulfill the will of the deceased; and if there be nothing due

from him to us, all the chattels shall go to the deceased, saving to his wife and children their reasonable shares.

27. If any freeman shall die intestate, his chattels shall be distributed by the hands of his nearest kinsfolk and friends, under supervision of the Church, saving to everyone the debts which the deceased owed to him.

28. No constable or other bailiff of ours shall take corn or other provisions from anyone without immediately tendering money therefor, unless he can have postponement thereof by permission of the seller.

29. No constable shall compel any knight to give money in lieu of castle-guard, when he is willing to perform it in his own person, or (if he himself cannot do it from any reasonable cause) then by another responsible man. Further, if we have led or sent him upon military service, he shall be relieved from guard in proportion to the time during which he has been on service because of us.

30. No sheriff or bailiff of ours, or other person, shall take the horses or carts of any freeman for transport duty, against the will of the said freeman.

31. Neither we nor our bailiffs shall take, for our castles or for any other work of ours, wood which

is not ours, against the will of the owner of that wood.

32. We will not retain beyond one year and one day, the lands those who have been convicted of felony, and the lands shall thereafter be handed over to the lords of the fiefs.

33. All kydells for the future shall be removed altogether from Thames and Medway, and throughout all England, except upon the seashore.

34. The writ which is called praecipe shall not for the future be issued to anyone, regarding any tenement whereby a freeman may lose his court.

35. Let there be one measure of wine throughout our whole realm; and one measure of ale; and one measure of corn, to wit, "the London quarter"; and one width of cloth (whether dyed, or russet, or "halberget"), to wit, two ells within the selvedges; of weights also let it be as of measures.

36. Nothing in future shall be given or taken for a writ of inquisition of life or limbs, but freely it shall be granted, and never denied.

37. If anyone holds of us by fee-farm, either by socage or by burage, or of any other land by knight's service, we will not (by reason of that fee-farm, socage, or burgage), have the wardship of the heir, or of such land of his as if of the fief of that other; nor shall we have wardship of that fee-

farm, socage, or burgage, unless such fee-farm owes knight's service. We will not by reason of any small serjeancy which anyone may hold of us by the service of rendering to us knives, arrows, or the like, have wardship of his heir or of the land which he holds of another lord by knight's service.

38. No bailiff for the future shall, upon his own unsupported complaint, put anyone to his "law", without credible witnesses brought for this purposes.

39. No freemen shall be taken or imprisoned or disseised or exiled or in any way destroyed, nor will we go upon him nor send upon him, except by the lawful judgment of his peers or by the law of the land.

40. To no one will we sell, to no one will we refuse or delay, right or justice.

41. All merchants shall have safe and secure exit from England, and entry to England, with the right to tarry there and to move about as well by land as by water, for buying and selling by the ancient and right customs, quit from all evil tolls, except (in time of war) such merchants as are of the land at war with us. And if such are found in our land at the beginning of the war, they shall be detained, without injury to their bodies or goods, until information be received by us, or by our chief justiciar, how the merchants of our land found in

the land at war with us are treated; and if our men are safe there, the others shall be safe in our land.

42. It shall be lawful in future for anyone (excepting always those imprisoned or outlawed in accordance with the law of the kingdom, and natives of any country at war with us, and merchants, who shall be treated as if above provided) to leave our kingdom and to return, safe and secure by land and water, except for a short period in time of war, on grounds of public policy-reserving always the allegiance due to us.

43. If anyone holding of some escheat (such as the honor of Wallingford, Nottingham, Boulogne, Lancaster, or of other escheats which are in our hands and are baronies) shall die, his heir shall give no other relief, and perform no other service to us than he would have done to the baron if that barony had been in the baron's hand; and we shall hold it in the same manner in which the baron held it.

44. Men who dwell without the forest need not henceforth come before our justiciaries of the forest upon a general summons, unless they are in plea, or sureties of one or more, who are attached for the forest.

45. We will appoint as justices, constables, sheriffs, or bailiffs only such as know the law of the realm and mean to observe it well.

46. All barons who have founded abbeys, concerning which they hold charters from the kings of England, or of which they have long continued possession, shall have the wardship of them, when vacant, as they ought to have.

47. All forests that have been made such in our time shall forthwith be disafforsted; and a similar course shall be followed with regard to river banks that have been placed "in defense" by us in our time.

48. All evil customs connected with forests and warrens, foresters and warreners, sheriffs and their officers, river banks and their wardens, shall immediately by inquired into in each county by twelve sworn knights of the same county chosen by the honest men of the same county, and shall, within forty days of the said inquest, be utterly abolished, so as never to be restored, provided always that we previously have intimation thereof, or our justiciar, if we should not be in England.

49. We will immediately restore all hostages and charters delivered to us by Englishmen, as sureties of the peace of faithful service.

50. We will entirely remove from their bailiwicks, the relations of Gerard of Athee (so that in future they shall have no bailiwick in England); namely, Engelard of Cigogne, Peter, Guy, and Andrew of Chanceaux, Guy of Cigogne, Geoffrey of Martigny with his brothers, Philip Mark with his

brothers and his nephew Geoffrey, and the whole brood of the same.

51. As soon as peace is restored, we will banish from the kingdom all foreign born knights, crossbowmen, serjeants, and mercenary soldiers who have come with horses and arms to the kingdom's hurt.

52. If anyone has been dispossessed or removed by us, without the legal judgment of his peers, from his lands, castles, franchises, or from his right, we will immediately restore them to him; and if a dispute arise over this, then let it be decided by the five and twenty barons of whom mention is made below in the clause for securing the peace. Moreover, for all those possessions, from which anyone has, without the lawful judgment of his peers, been disseised or removed, by our father, King Henry, or by our brother, King Richard, and which we retain in our hand (or which as possessed by others, to whom we are bound to warrant them) we shall have respite until the usual term of crusaders; excepting those things about which a plea has been raised, or an inquest made by our order, before our taking of the cross; but as soon as we return from the expedition, we will immediately grant full justice therein.

53. We shall have, moreover, the same respite and in the same manner in rendering justice concerning the disafforestation or retention of those forests which Henry our father and Richard

our broter afforested, and concerning the wardship of lands which are of the fief of another (namely, such wardships as we have hitherto had by reason of a fief which anyone held of us by knight's service), and concerning abbeys founded on other fiefs than our own, in which the lord of the fee claims to have right; and when we have returned, or if we desist from our expedition, we will immediately grant full justice to all who complain of such things.

54. No one shall be arrested or imprisoned upon the appeal of a woman, for the death of any other than her husband.

55. All fines made with us unjustly and against the law of the land, and all amercements, imposed unjustly and against the law of the land, shall be entirely remitted, or else it shall be done concerning them according to the decision of the five and twenty barons whom mention is made below in the clause for securing the pease, or according to the judgment of the majority of the same, along with the aforesaid Stephen, archbishop of Canterbury, if he can be present, and such others as he may wish to bring with him for this purpose, and if he cannot be present the business shall nevertheless proceed without him, provided always that if any one or more of the aforesaid five and twenty barons are in a similar suit, they shall be removed as far as concerns this particular judgment, others being substituted in their places after having been selected by the rest

of the same five and twenty for this purpose only, and after having been sworn.

56. If we have disseised or removed Welshmen from lands or liberties, or other things, without the legal judgment of their peers in England or in Wales, they shall be immediately restored to them; and if a dispute arise over this, then let it be decided in the marches by the judgment of their peers; for the tenements in England according to the law of England, for tenements in Wales according to the law of Wales, and for tenements in the marches according to the law of the marches. Welshmen shall do the same to us and ours.

57. Further, for all those possessions from which any Welshman has, without the lawful judgment of his peers, been disseised or removed by King Henry our father, or King Richard our brother, and which we retain in our hand (or which are possessed by others, and which we ought to warrant), we will have respite until the usual term of crusaders; excepting those things about which a plea has been raised or an inquest made by our order before we took the cross; but as soon as we return (or if perchance we desist from our expedition), we will immediately grant full justice in accordance with the laws of the Welsh and in relation to the foresaid regions.

58. We will immediately give up the son of Llywelyn and all the hostages of Wales, and the charters delivered to us as security for the peace.

59. We will do towards Alexander, king of Scots, concerning the return of his sisters and his hostages, and concerning his franchises, and his right, in the same manner as we shall do towards our owher barons of England, unless it ought to be otherwise according to the charters which we hold from William his father, formerly king of Scots; and this shall be according to the judgment of his peers in our court.

60. Moreover, all these aforesaid customs and liberties, the observances of which we have granted in our kingdom as far as pertains to us towards our men, shall be observed b all of our kingdom, as well clergy as laymen, as far as pertains to them towards their men.

61. Since, moveover, for God and the amendment of our kingdom and for the better allaying of the quarrel that has arisen between us and our barons, we have granted all these concessions, desirous that they should enjoy them in complete and firm endurance forever, we give and grant to them the underwritten security, namely, that the barons choose five and twenty barons of the kingdom, whomsoever they will, who shall be bound with all their might, to observe and hold, and cause to be observed, the peace and liberties we have granted and confirmed to them by this our present

Charter, so that if we, or our justiciar, or our bailiffs or any one of our officers, shall in anything be at fault towards anyone, or shall have broken any one of the articles of this peace or of this security, and the offense be notified to four barons of the foresaid five and twenty, the said four barons shall repair to us (or our justiciar, if we are out of the realm) and, laying the transgression before us, petition to have that transgression redressed without delay. And if we shall not have corrected the transgression (or, in the event of our being out of the realm, if our justiciar shall not have corrected it) within forty days, reckoning from the time it has been intimated to us (or to our justiciar, if we should be out of the realm), the four barons aforesaid shall refer that matter to the rest of the five and twenty barons, and those five and twenty barons shall, together with the community of the whole realm, distrain and distress us in all possible ways, namely, by seizing our castles, lands, possessions, and in any other way they can, until redress has been obtained as they deem fit, saving harmless our own person, and the persons of our queen and children; and when redress has been obtained, they shall resume their old relations towards us. And let whoever in the country desires it, swear to obey the orders of the said five and twenty barons for the execution of all the aforesaid matters, and along with them, to molest us to the utmost of his power; and we publicly and freely grant leave to everyone who wishes to swear, and we shall never forbid anyone to swear. All those, moveover, in the land who of themselves and of their own accord are unwilling to swear to the twenty five to help them in constraining and molesting us, we shall by our command compel the same to swear to the effect foresaid. And if any one of the five and twenty barons shall have died or departed from the land, or be incapacitated in any other manner which would prevent the foresaid provisions being carried out, those of the said twenty five barons who are left shall choose another in his place according to their own judgment, and he shall be sworn in the same way as the others. Further, in all matters, the execution of which is entrusted,to these twenty five barons, if perchance these twenty five are present and disagree about anything, or if some of them, after being summoned, are unwilling or unable to be present, that which the majority of those present ordain or command shall be held as fixed and established, exactly as if the whole twenty five had concurred in this; and the said twenty five shall swear that they will faithfully observe all that is aforesaid, and cause it to be observed with all their might. And we shall procure nothing from anyone, directly or indirectly, whereby any part of these concessions and liberties might be revoked or diminished; and if any such things has been procured, let it be void and null, and we shall never use it personally or by another.

62. And all the will, hatreds, and bitterness that have arisen between us and our men, clergy and lay, from the date of the quarrel, we have

completely remitted and pardoned to everyone. Moreover, all trespasses occasioned by the said quarrel, from Easter in the sixteenth year of our reign till the restoration of peace, we have fully remitted to all, both clergy and laymen, and completely forgiven, as far as pertains to us. And on this head, we have caused to be made for them letters testimonial patent of the lord Stephen, archbishop of Canterbury, of the lord Henry, archbishop of Dublin, of the bishops aforesaid, and of Master Pandulf as touching this security and the concessions aforesaid.

63. Wherefore we will and firmly order that the English Church be free, and that the men in our kingdom have and hold all the aforesaid liberties, rights, and concessions, well and peaceably, freely and quietly, fully and wholly, for themselves and their heirs, of us and our heirs, in all respects and in all places forever, as is aforesaid. An oath, moreover, has been taken, as well on our part as on the art of the barons, that all these conditions aforesaid shall be kept in good faith and without evil intent.

Given under our hand - the above named and many others being witnesses - in the meadow which is called Runnymede, between Windsor and Staines, on the fifteenth day of June, in the seventeenth year of our reign.

Declaration of the Rights of Man and Citizen

Approved by the National Assembly of France, August 26, 1789

The representatives of the French people, organized as a National Assembly, believing that the ignorance, neglect, or contempt of the rights of man are the sole cause of public calamities and of the corruption of governments, have determined to set forth in a solemn declaration the natural, unalienable, and sacred rights of man, in order that this declaration, being constantly before all the members of the Social body, shall remind them continually of their rights and duties; in order that the acts of the legislative power, as well as those of the executive power, may be compared at any moment with the objects and purposes of all political institutions and may thus be more respected, and, lastly, in order that the grievances of the citizens, based hereafter upon simple and incontestable principles, shall tend to the maintenance of the constitution and redound to the happiness of all. Therefore the National Assembly recognizes and proclaims, in the presence and under the auspices of the Supreme Being, the following rights of man and of the citizen:

Articles:

1. Men are born and remain free and equal in rights. Social distinctions may be founded only upon the general good.

2. The aim of all political association is the preservation of the natural and imprescriptible rights of man. These rights are liberty, property, security, and resistance to oppression.

3. The principle of all sovereignty resides essentially in the nation. No body nor individual may exercise any authority which does not proceed directly from the nation.

4. Liberty consists in the freedom to do everything which injures no one else; hence the exercise of the natural rights of each man has no limits except those which assure to the other members of the society the enjoyment of the same rights. These limits can only be determined by law.

5. Law can only prohibit such actions as are hurtful to society. Nothing may be prevented which is not forbidden by law, and no one may be forced to do anything not provided for by law.

6. Law is the expression of the general will. Every citizen has a right to participate personally, or through his representative, in its foundation. It must be the same for all, whether it protects or

punishes. All citizens, being equal in the eyes of the law, are equally eligible to all dignities and to all public positions and occupations, according to their abilities, and without distinction except that of their virtues and talents.

7. No person shall be accused, arrested, or imprisoned except in the cases and according to the forms prescribed by law. Any one soliciting, transmitting, executing, or causing to be executed, any arbitrary order, shall be punished. But any citizen summoned or arrested in virtue of the law shall submit without delay, as resistance constitutes an offense.

8. The law shall provide for such punishments only as are strictly and obviously necessary, and no one shall suffer punishment except it be legally inflicted in virtue of a law passed and promulgated before the commission of the offense.

9. As all persons are held innocent until they shall have been declared guilty, if arrest shall be deemed indispensable, all harshness not essential to the securing of the prisoner's person shall be severely repressed by law.

10. No one shall be disquieted on account of his opinions, including his religious views, provided their manifestation does not disturb the public order established by law.

11. The free communication of ideas and opinions is one of the most precious of the rights of man. Every citizen may, accordingly, speak, write, and print with freedom, but shall be responsible for such abuses of this freedom as shall be defined by law.

12. The security of the rights of man and of the citizen requires public military forces. These forces are, therefore, established for the good of all and not for the personal advantage of those to whom they shall be intrusted.

13. A common contribution is essential for the maintenance of the public forces and for the cost of administration. This should be equitably distributed among all the citizens in proportion to their means.

14. All the citizens have a right to decide, either personally or by their representatives, as to the necessity of the public contribution; to grant this freely; to know to what uses it is put; and to fix the proportion, the mode of assessment and of collection and the duration of the taxes.

15. Society has the right to require of every public agent an account of his administration.

16. A society in which the observance of the law is not assured, nor the separation of powers defined, has no constitution at all.

17. Since property is an inviolable and sacred right, no one shall be deprived thereof except where public necessity, legally determined, shall clearly demand it, and then only on condition that the owner shall have been previously and equitably indemnified.

Bibliographical information
Alexis Francois Pison de Galland, 1747-1826
Declaration des droits de l'homme et du citoyen / par A.F. Pison du Galland, membre de l'Assemble nationale
Imprint: *A Versailles: Chez Baudoin . . . .,* [1789]
(New York Public Library Rare Book Room Call Numbers: KVR KVR 3021; KVR 3022 and KVR 11175)

The above document was written by The Marquis de Lafayette, with help from his friend and neighbor, American envoy to France, Thomas Jefferson. There are also versions credited to Alexis Francois Pison de Galland, a member of the National Assembly who approved the Declaration (hence the bibliographical information). Lafayette had come to the Colonies at age 19, been commissioned a Major General, and was instrumental in the defeat of the British during the American Revolutionary War. He considered one special man his 'father': George Washington.

THE CONSTITUTION OF THE UNITED STATES

Preamble

WE THE PEOPLE of the United States, in Order to form a more perfect Union, establish Justice, insure domestic Tranquility, provide for the common defence, promote the general Welfare, and secure the Blessings of Liberty to ourselves and our Posterity, do ordain and establish this Constitution for the United States of America.

Article. I. - The Legislative Branch

Section 1 - The Legislature

All legislative Powers herein granted shall be vested in a Congress of the United States, which shall consist of a Senate and House of Representatives.

Section 2 - The House

The House of Representatives shall be composed of Members chosen every second Year by the People of the several States, and the Electors in each State shall have the Qualifications requisite for Electors of the most numerous Branch of the State Legislature.

No Person shall be a Representative who shall not have attained to the Age of twenty five Years, and been seven Years a Citizen of the United States, and who shall not, when elected, be an Inhabitant of that State in which he shall be chosen.

(Representatives and direct Taxes shall be apportioned among the several States which may be included within this Union, according to their respective Numbers, which shall be determined by adding to the whole Number of free Persons, including those bound to Service for a Term of Years, and excluding Indians not taxed, three fifths of all other Persons.) **(The previous**

sentence in parentheses was modified by the 14th Amendment, section 2.) The actual Enumeration shall be made within three Years after the first Meeting of the Congress of the United States, and within every subsequent Term of ten Years, in such Manner as they shall by Law direct. The Number of Representatives shall not exceed one for every thirty Thousand, but each State shall have at Least one Representative; and until such enumeration shall be made, the State of New Hampshire shall be entitled to chuse three, Massachusetts eight, Rhode Island and Providence Plantations one, Connecticut five, New York six, New Jersey four, Pennsylvania eight, Delaware one, Maryland six, Virginia ten, North Carolina five, South Carolina five and Georgia three.

When vacancies happen in the Representation from any State, the Executive Authority thereof shall issue Writs of Election to fill such Vacancies.

The House of Representatives shall chuse their Speaker and other Officers; and shall have the sole Power of Impeachment.

Section 3 - The Senate

The Senate of the United States shall be composed of two Senators from each State, *(chosen by the Legislature thereof,)* **(The preceding words in parentheses superseded by 17th Amendment, section 1.)** for six Years; and each Senator shall have one Vote.

Immediately after they shall be assembled in Consequence of the first Election, they shall be divided as equally as may be into three Classes. The Seats of the Senators of the first Class shall be vacated at the Expiration of the second Year, of the second Class at the Expiration of the fourth Year, and of the third Class at the Expiration of the sixth Year, so that one third may be chosen every second Year; *(and if Vacancies happen by Resignation, or otherwise, during the Recess of the Legislature of any State, the Executive thereof may make temporary Appointments until the next Meeting of the Legislature, which shall then fill such Vacancies.)* **(The preceding words in parentheses were superseded by the 17th Amendment, section 2.)**

No person shall be a Senator who shall not have attained to the Age of thirty Years, and been nine Years a Citizen of the United States, and who shall not, when elected, be an Inhabitant of that State for which he shall be chosen.

The Vice President of the United States shall be President of the Senate, but shall have no Vote, unless they be equally divided.

The Senate shall chuse their other Officers, and also a President pro tempore, in the absence of the Vice President, or when he shall exercise the Office of President of the United States.

The Senate shall have the sole Power to try all Impeachments. When sitting for that Purpose, they shall be on Oath or Affirmation. When the President of the United States is tried, the Chief Justice shall preside: And no Person shall be convicted without the Concurrence of two thirds of the Members present.

Judgment in Cases of Impeachment shall not extend further than to removal from Office, and disqualification to hold and enjoy any Office of honor, Trust or Profit under the United States: but the Party convicted shall nevertheless be liable and subject to Indictment, Trial, Judgment and Punishment, according to Law.

Section 4 - Elections, Meetings

The Times, Places and Manner of holding Elections for Senators and Representatives, shall be prescribed in each State by the Legislature thereof; but the Congress may at any time by Law make or alter such Regulations, except as to the Place of Chusing Senators.

The Congress shall assemble at least once in every Year, and such Meeting shall *(be on the first Monday in December,)* **(The preceding words in parentheses were superseded by the 20th Amendment, section 2.)** unless they shall by Law appoint a different Day.

Section 5 - Membership, Rules, Journals, Adjournment

Each House shall be the Judge of the Elections, Returns and Qualifications of its own Members, and a Majority of each shall constitute a Quorum to do Business; but a smaller number may adjourn from day to day, and may be authorized to compel the Attendance of absent Members, in such Manner, and under such Penalties as each House may provide.

Each House may determine the Rules of its Proceedings, punish its Members for disorderly Behavior, and, with the Concurrence of two-thirds, expel a Member.

Each House shall keep a Journal of its Proceedings, and from time to time publish the same, excepting such Parts as may in their Judgment require Secrecy; and the Yeas and Nays of the Members of either House on any question shall, at the Desire of one fifth of those Present, be entered on the Journal.

Neither House, during the Session of Congress, shall, without the Consent of the other, adjourn for more than three days, nor to any other Place than that in which the two Houses shall be sitting.

Section 6 - Compensation

(The Senators and Representatives shall receive a Compensation for their Services, to be ascertained by Law, and paid out of the Treasury of the United

States.) **(The preceding words in parentheses were modified by the 27th Amendment.)** They shall in all Cases, except Treason, Felony and Breach of the Peace, be privileged from Arrest during their Attendance at the Session of their respective Houses, and in going to and returning from the same; and for any Speech or Debate in either House, they shall not be questioned in any other Place.

No Senator or Representative shall, during the Time for which he was elected, be appointed to any civil Office under the Authority of the United States which shall have been created, or the Emoluments whereof shall have been increased during such time; and no Person holding any Office under the United States, shall be a Member of either House during his Continuance in Office.

Section 7 - Revenue Bills, Legislative Process, Presidential Veto

All bills for raising Revenue shall originate in the House of Representatives; but the Senate may propose or concur with Amendments as on other Bills.

Every Bill which shall have passed the House of Representatives and the Senate, shall, before it become a Law, be presented to the President of the United States; If he approve he shall sign it, but if not he shall return it, with his Objections to that House in which it shall have originated, who shall enter the Objections at large on their Journal, and proceed to reconsider it. If after such Reconsideration two thirds of that House shall agree to pass the Bill, it shall be sent, together with the Objections, to the other House, by which it shall likewise be reconsidered, and if approved by two thirds of that House, it shall become a Law. But in all such Cases the Votes of both Houses shall be determined by Yeas and Nays, and the Names of the Persons voting for and against the Bill shall be entered on the Journal of each House respectively. If any Bill shall not be returned by the President within ten Days (Sundays excepted) after it shall have been presented to him, the Same shall be a Law, in like Manner as if he had signed it, unless the Congress by their Adjournment prevent its Return, in which Case it shall not be a Law.

Every Order, Resolution, or Vote to which the Concurrence of the Senate and House of Representatives may be necessary (except on a question of Adjournment) shall be presented to the President of the United States; and before the Same shall take Effect, shall be approved by him, or being disapproved by him, shall be repassed by two thirds of the Senate and House of Representatives, according to the Rules and Limitations prescribed in the Case of a Bill.

Section 8 - Powers of Congress

The Congress shall have Power To lay and collect Taxes, Duties, Imposts and Excises, to pay the Debts and provide for the common Defence and general Welfare of the United States; but all Duties, Imposts and Excises shall be uniform throughout the United States;

To borrow money on the credit of the United States;

To regulate Commerce with foreign Nations, and among the several States, and with the Indian Tribes;

To establish an uniform Rule of Naturalization, and uniform Laws on the subject of Bankruptcies throughout the United States;

To coin Money, regulate the Value thereof, and of foreign Coin, and fix the Standard of Weights and Measures;

To provide for the Punishment of counterfeiting the Securities and current Coin of the United States;

To establish Post Offices and Post Roads;

To promote the Progress of Science and useful Arts, by securing for limited Times to Authors and Inventors the exclusive Right to their respective

Writings and Discoveries; To constitute Tribunals inferior to the supreme Court;

To define and punish Piracies and Felonies committed on the high Seas, and Offenses against the Law of Nations;

To declare War, grant Letters of Marque and Reprisal, and make Rules concerning Captures on Land and Water;

To raise and support Armies, but no Appropriation of Money to that Use shall be for a longer Term than two Years;

To provide and maintain a Navy;

To make Rules for the Government and Regulation of the land and naval Forces;

To provide for calling forth the Militia to execute the Laws of the Union, suppress Insurrections and repel Invasions;

To provide for organizing, arming, and disciplining the Militia, and for governing such Part of them as may be employed in the Service of the United States, reserving to the States respectively, the Appointment of the Officers, and the Authority of training the Militia according to the discipline prescribed by Congress;

To exercise exclusive Legislation in all Cases

whatsoever, over such District (not exceeding ten Miles square) as may, by Cession of particular States, and the acceptance of Congress, become the Seat of the Government of the United States, and to exercise like Authority over all Places purchased by the Consent of the Legislature of the State in which the Same shall be, for the Erection of Forts, Magazines, Arsenals, dock-Yards, and other needful Buildings; And

To make all Laws which shall be necessary and proper for carrying into Execution the foregoing Powers, and all other Powers vested by this Constitution in the Government of the United States, or in any Department or Officer thereof.

Section 9 - Limits on Congress

The Migration or Importation of such Persons as any of the States now existing shall think proper to admit, shall not be prohibited by the Congress prior to the Year one thousand eight hundred and eight, but a tax or duty may be imposed on such Importation, not exceeding ten dollars for each Person.

The privilege of the Writ of Habeas Corpus shall not be suspended, unless when in Cases of Rebellion or Invasion the public Safety may require it.

No Bill of Attainder or ex post facto Law shall be passed.

(No capitation, or other direct, Tax shall be laid, unless in Proportion to the Census or Enumeration herein before directed to be taken.) **(Section in parentheses clarified by the 16th Amendment.)**

No Tax or Duty shall be laid on Articles exported from any State.

No Preference shall be given by any Regulation of Commerce or Revenue to the Ports of one State over those of another: nor shall Vessels bound to, or from, one State, be obliged to enter, clear, or pay Duties in another.

No Money shall be drawn from the Treasury, but in Consequence of Appropriations made by Law; and a regular Statement and Account of the Receipts and Expenditures of all public Money shall be published from time to time.

No Title of Nobility shall be granted by the United States: And no Person holding any Office of Profit or Trust under them, shall, without the Consent of the Congress, accept of any present, Emolument, Office, or Title, of any kind whatever, from any King, Prince or foreign State.

Section 10 - Powers prohibited of States

No State shall enter into any Treaty, Alliance, or Confederation; grant Letters of Marque and Reprisal; coin Money; emit Bills of Credit; make any Thing but gold and silver Coin a Tender in Payment of Debts; pass any Bill of Attainder, ex post facto Law, or Law impairing the Obligation of Contracts, or grant any Title of Nobility.

No State shall, without the Consent of the Congress, lay any Imposts or Duties on Imports or Exports, except what may be absolutely necessary for executing it's inspection Laws: and the net Produce of all Duties and Imposts, laid by any State on Imports or Exports, shall be for the Use of the Treasury of the United States; and all such Laws shall be subject to the Revision and Controul of the Congress.

No State shall, without the Consent of Congress, lay any duty of Tonnage, keep Troops, or Ships of War in time of Peace, enter into any Agreement or Compact with another State, or with a foreign Power, or engage in War, unless actually invaded, or in such imminent Danger as will not admit of delay.

Article. II. - The Executive Branch

Section 1 - The President

The executive Power shall be vested in a President of the United States of America. He shall hold his Office during the Term of four Years, and, together with the Vice-President chosen for the same Term, be elected, as follows:

Each State shall appoint, in such Manner as the Legislature thereof may direct, a Number of Electors, equal to the whole Number of Senators and Representatives to which the State may be entitled in the Congress: but no Senator or Representative, or Person holding an Office of Trust or Profit under the United States, shall be appointed an Elector.

(The Electors shall meet in their respective States, and vote by Ballot for two persons, of whom one at least shall not lie an Inhabitant of the same State with themselves. And they shall make a List of all the Persons voted for, and of the Number of Votes for each; which List they shall sign and certify, and transmit sealed to the Seat of the Government of the United States, directed to the President of the Senate. The President of the Senate shall, in the Presence of the Senate and House of Representatives, open all the Certificates, and the Votes shall then be counted. The Person having the greatest Number of Votes

shall be the President, if such Number be a Majority of the whole Number of Electors appointed; and if there be more than one who have such Majority, and have an equal Number of Votes, then the House of Representatives shall immediately chuse by Ballot one of them for President; and if no Person have a Majority, then from the five highest on the List the said House shall in like Manner chuse the President. But in chusing the President, the Votes shall be taken by States, the Representation from each State having one Vote; a quorum for this Purpose shall consist of a Member or Members from two-thirds of the States, and a Majority of all the States shall be necessary to a Choice. In every Case, after the Choice of the President, the Person having the greatest Number of Votes of the Electors shall be the Vice President. But if there should remain two or more who have equal Votes, the Senate shall chuse from them by Ballot the Vice-President.) **(This clause in parentheses was superseded by the 12th Amendment.)**

The Congress may determine the Time of chusing the Electors, and the Day on which they shall give their Votes; which Day shall be the same throughout the United States.

No person except a natural born Citizen, or a Citizen of the United States, at the time of the Adoption of this Constitution, shall be eligible to the Office of President; neither shall any Person be eligible to that Office who shall not have attained to the Age of thirty-five Years, and been fourteen Years a Resident within the United States.

(In Case of the Removal of the President from Office, or of his Death, Resignation, or Inability to discharge the Powers and Duties of the said Office, the same shall devolve on the Vice President, and the Congress may by Law provide for the Case of Removal, Death, Resignation or Inability, both of the President and Vice President, declaring what Officer shall then act as President, and such Officer shall act accordingly, until the Disability be removed, or a President shall be elected.) **(This clause in parentheses has been modified by the 20th and 25th Amendments.)**

The President shall, at stated Times, receive for his Services, a Compensation, which shall neither be increased nor diminished during the Period for which he shall have been elected, and he shall not receive within that Period any other Emolument from the United States, or any of them.

Before he enter on the Execution of his Office, he shall take the following Oath or Affirmation:

"I do solemnly swear (or affirm) that I will faithfully execute the Office of President of the United States, and will to the best of my Ability, preserve, protect and defend the Constitution of the United States."

Section 2 - Civilian Power over Military,

Cabinet, Pardon Power, Appointments

The President shall be Commander in Chief of the Army and Navy of the United States, and of the Militia of the several States, when called into the actual Service of the United States; he may require the Opinion, in writing, of the principal Officer in each of the executive Departments, upon any subject relating to the Duties of their respective Offices, and he shall have Power to Grant Reprieves and Pardons for Offenses against the United States, except in Cases of Impeachment.

He shall have Power, by and with the Advice and Consent of the Senate, to make Treaties, provided two thirds of the Senators present concur; and he shall nominate, and by and with the Advice and Consent of the Senate, shall appoint Ambassadors, other public Ministers and Consuls, Judges of the supreme Court, and all other Officers of the United States, whose Appointments are not herein otherwise provided for, and which shall be established by Law: but the Congress may by Law vest the Appointment of such inferior Officers, as they think proper, in the President alone, in the Courts of Law, or in the Heads of Departments.

The President shall have Power to fill up all Vacancies that may happen during the Recess of the Senate, by granting Commissions which shall expire at the End of their next Session.

Section 3 - State of the Union, Convening Congress

He shall from time to time give to the Congress Information of the State of the Union, and recommend to their Consideration such Measures as he shall judge necessary and expedient; he may, on extraordinary Occasions, convene both Houses, or either of them, and in Case of Disagreement between them, with Respect to the Time of Adjournment, he may adjourn them to such Time as he shall think proper; he shall receive Ambassadors and other public Ministers; he shall take Care that the Laws be faithfully executed, and shall Commission all the Officers of the United States.

Section 4 - Disqualification

The President, Vice President and all civil Officers of the United States, shall be removed from Office on Impeachment for, and Conviction of, Treason, Bribery, or other high Crimes and Misdemeanors.

Article III. - The Judicial Branch

Section 1 - Judicial powers

The judicial Power of the United States, shall be vested in one supreme Court, and in such inferior Courts as the Congress may from time to time ordain and establish. The Judges, both of the supreme and inferior Courts, shall hold their Offices during good Behavior, and shall, at stated Times, receive for their Services a Compensation which shall not be diminished during their Continuance in Office.

Section 2 - Trial by Jury, Original Jurisdiction, Jury Trials

(The judicial Power shall extend to all Cases, in Law and Equity, arising under this Constitution, the Laws of the United States, and Treaties made, or which shall be made, under their Authority; to all Cases affecting Ambassadors, other public Ministers and Consuls; to all Cases of admiralty and maritime Jurisdiction; to Controversies to which the United States shall be a Party; to Controversies between two or more States; between a State and Citizens of another State; between Citizens of different States; between Citizens of the same State claiming Lands under Grants of different States, and between a State, or the Citizens thereof, and foreign States, Citizens

or Subjects.) **(This section in parentheses is modified by the 11th Amendment.)**

In all Cases affecting Ambassadors, other public Ministers and Consuls, and those in which a State shall be Party, the supreme Court shall have original Jurisdiction. In all the other Cases before mentioned, the supreme Court shall have appellate Jurisdiction, both as to Law and Fact, with such Exceptions, and under such Regulations as the Congress shall make.

The Trial of all Crimes, except in Cases of Impeachment, shall be by Jury; and such Trial shall be held in the State where the said Crimes shall have been committed; but when not committed within any State, the Trial shall be at such Place or Places as the Congress may by Law have directed.

Section 3 - Treason

Treason against the United States, shall consist only in levying War against them, or in adhering to their Enemies, giving them Aid and Comfort. No Person shall be convicted of Treason unless on the Testimony of two Witnesses to the same overt Act, or on Confession in open Court.

The Congress shall have power to declare the Punishment of Treason, but no Attainder of Treason shall work Corruption of Blood, or Forfeiture except during the Life of the Person attainted.

Article. IV. - The States

Section 1 - Each State to Honor all others

Full Faith and Credit shall be given in each State to the public Acts, Records, and judicial Proceedings of every other State. And the Congress may by general Laws prescribe the Manner in which such Acts, Records and Proceedings shall be proved, and the Effect thereof.

Section 2 - State citizens, Extradition

The Citizens of each State shall be entitled to all Privileges and Immunities of Citizens in the several States.

A Person charged in any State with Treason, Felony, or other Crime, who shall flee from Justice, and be found in another State, shall on demand of the executive Authority of the State from which he fled, be delivered up, to be removed to the State having Jurisdiction of the Crime.

(No Person held to Service or Labour in one State, under the Laws thereof, escaping into another, shall, in Consequence of any Law or Regulation therein, be discharged from such Service or Labour, But shall be delivered up on Claim of the Party to whom such Service or Labour may be

due.) **(This clause in parentheses is superseded by the 13th Amendment.)**

Section 3 - New States

New States may be admitted by the Congress into this Union; but no new States shall be formed or erected within the Jurisdiction of any other State; nor any State be formed by the Junction of two or more States, or parts of States, without the Consent of the Legislatures of the States concerned as well as of the Congress.

The Congress shall have Power to dispose of and make all needful Rules and Regulations respecting the Territory or other Property belonging to the United States; and nothing in this Constitution shall be so construed as to Prejudice any Claims of the United States, or of any particular State.

Section 4 - Republican government

The United States shall guarantee to every State in this Union a Republican Form of Government, and shall protect each of them against Invasion; and on Application of the Legislature, or of the Executive (when the Legislature cannot be convened) against domestic Violence.

Article. V. - Amendment

The Congress, whenever two thirds of both Houses shall deem it necessary, shall propose Amendments to this Constitution, or, on the Application of the Legislatures of two thirds of the several States, shall call a Convention for proposing Amendments, which, in either Case, shall be valid to all Intents and Purposes, as part of this Constitution, when ratified by the Legislatures of three fourths of the several States, or by Conventions in three fourths thereof, as the one or the other Mode of Ratification may be proposed by the Congress; Provided that no Amendment which may be made prior to the Year One thousand eight hundred and eight shall in any Manner affect the first and fourth Clauses in the Ninth Section of the first Article; and that no State, without its Consent, shall be deprived of its equal Suffrage in the Senate.

Article. VI. - Debts, Supremacy, Oaths

All Debts contracted and Engagements entered into, before the Adoption of this Constitution, shall be as valid against the United States under this Constitution, as under the Confederation.

This Constitution, and the Laws of the United States which shall be made in Pursuance thereof; and all Treaties made, or which shall be made, under the Authority of the United States, shall be the supreme Law of the Land; and the Judges in every State shall be bound thereby, any Thing in the Constitution or Laws of any State to the Contrary notwithstanding.

The Senators and Representatives before mentioned, and the Members of the several State Legislatures, and all executive and judicial Officers, both of the United States and of the several States, shall be bound by Oath or Affirmation, to support this Constitution; but no religious Test shall ever be required as a Qualification to any Office or public Trust under the United States.

Article. VII. - Ratification

The Ratification of the Conventions of nine States, shall be sufficient for the Establishment of this Constitution between the States so ratifying the Same.

Done in Convention by the Unanimous Consent of the States present the Seventeenth Day of September in the Year of our Lord one thousand seven hundred and Eighty seven and of the Independence of the United States of America the Twelfth. In Witness whereof We have hereunto subscribed our Names.

Go Washington - President and deputy from Virginia New Hampshire - John Langdon, Nicholas Gilman Massachusetts - Nathaniel Gorham, Rufus King Connecticut - Wm Saml Johnson, Roger Sherman New York - Alexander Hamilton
New Jersey - Wil Livingston, David Brearley, Wm Paterson, Jona. Dayton

Pensylvania - B Franklin, Thomas Mifflin, Robt Morris, Geo. Clymer, Thos FitzSimons, Jared Ingersoll, James Wilson, Gouv Morris

Delaware - Geo. Read, Gunning Bedford jun, John Dickinson, Richard Bassett, Jaco. Broom

Maryland - James McHenry, Dan of St Tho

Jenifer, Danl Carroll Virginia - John Blair, James Madison Jr.

North Carolina - Wm Blount, Richd Dobbs Spaight, Hu Williamson

South Carolina - J. Rutledge, Charles Cotesworth Pinckney, Charles Pinckney, Pierce Butler

Georgia - William Few, Abr Baldwin Attest: William Jackson, Secretary

THE AMENDMENTS

The following are the Amendments to the Constitution. The first ten Amendments collectively are commonly known as the Bill of Rights.

Amendment 1 - Freedom of Religion, Press, Expression. Ratified 12/15/1791.

Congress shall make no law respecting an establishment of religion, or prohibiting the free exercise thereof; or abridging the freedom of speech, or of the press; or the right of the people peaceably to assemble, and to petition the Government for a redress of grievances.

Amendment 2 - Right to Bear Arms. Ratified 12/15/1791.

A well regulated Militia, being necessary to the security of a free State, the right of the people to keep and bear Arms, shall not be infringed.

Amendment 3 - Quartering of Soldiers. Ratified 12/15/1791.

No Soldier shall, in time of peace be quartered in any house, without the consent of the Owner, nor in time of war, but in a manner to be prescribed by law.

Amendment 4 - Search and Seizure. Ratified 12/15/1791.

The right of the people to be secure in their persons, houses, papers, and effects, against unreasonable searches and seizures, shall not be violated, and no Warrants shall issue, but upon probable cause, supported by Oath or affirmation, and particularly describing the place to be searched, and the persons or things to be seized.

Amendment 5 - Trial and Punishment, Compensation for Takings. Ratified 12/15/1791.

No person shall be held to answer for a capital, or otherwise infamous crime, unless on a presentment or indictment of a Grand Jury, except in cases arising in the land or naval forces, or in the Militia, when in actual service in time of War or public danger; nor shall any person be subject for the same offense to be twice put in jeopardy of life or limb; nor shall be compelled in any criminal case to be a witness against himself, nor be deprived of life, liberty, or property, without due process of law; nor shall private property be taken for public use, without just compensation.

Amendment 6 - Right to Speedy Trial, Confrontation of Witnesses. Ratified 12/15/1791.

In all criminal prosecutions, the accused shall enjoy the right to a speedy and public trial, by an impartial jury of the State and district wherein the crime shall have been committed, which district shall have been previously ascertained by law, and to be informed of the nature and cause of the accusation; to be confronted with the witnesses against him; to have compulsory process for obtaining witnesses in his favor, and to have the Assistance of Counsel for his defence.

Amendment 7 - Trial by Jury in Civil Cases. Ratified 12/15/1791.

In Suits at common law, where the value in controversy shall exceed twenty dollars, the right of trial by jury shall be preserved, and no fact tried by a jury, shall be otherwise re- examined in any Court of the United States, than according to the rules of the common law.

Amendment 8 - Cruel and Unusual Punishment. Ratified 12/15/1791.

Excessive bail shall not be required, nor excessive

fines imposed, nor cruel and unusual punishments inflicted.

Amendment 9 - Construction of Constitution. Ratified 12/15/1791.

The enumeration in the Constitution, of certain rights, shall not be construed to deny or disparage others retained by the people.

Amendment 10 - Powers of the States and People. Ratified 12/15/1791.

The powers not delegated to the United States by the Constitution, nor prohibited by it to the States, are reserved to the States respectively, or to the people.

Amendment 11 - Judicial Limits. Ratified 2/7/1795.

The Judicial power of the United States shall not be construed to extend to any suit in law or equity, commenced or prosecuted against one of the United States by Citizens of another State, or by Citizens or Subjects of any Foreign State.

Amendment 12 - Choosing the President, Vice-President. Ratified 6/15/1804.

The Electors shall meet in their respective states,

and vote by ballot for President and Vice-President, one of whom, at least, shall not be an inhabitant of the same state with themselves; they shall name in their ballots the person voted for as President, and in distinct ballots the person voted for as Vice-President, and they shall make distinct lists of all persons voted for as President, and of all persons voted for as Vice-President and of the number of votes for each, which lists they shall sign and certify, and transmit sealed to the seat of the government of the United States, directed to the President of the Senate;

The President of the Senate shall, in the presence of the Senate and House of Representatives, open all the certificates and the votes shall then be counted;

The person having the greatest Number of votes for President, shall be the President, if such number be a majority of the whole number of Electors appointed; and if no person have such majority, then from the persons having the highest numbers not exceeding three on the list of those voted for as President, the House of Representatives shall choose immediately, by ballot, the President. But in choosing the President, the votes shall be taken by states, the representation from each state having one vote; a quorum for this purpose shall consist of a member or members from two-thirds of the states, and a majority of all the states shall be necessary to a choice. And if the House of Representatives shall not choose a President whenever the right of choice shall devolve upon them, before the fourth day of March next following, then the Vice-President shall act as President, as in the case of the death or other constitutional disability of the President.

The person having the greatest number of votes as Vice-President, shall be the Vice- President, if such number be a majority of the whole number of Electors appointed, and if no person have a majority, then from the two highest numbers on the list, the Senate shall choose the Vice-President; a quorum for the purpose shall consist of two-thirds of the whole number of Senators, and a majority of the whole number shall be necessary to a choice. But no person constitutionally ineligible to the office of President shall be eligible to that of Vice-President of the United States.

Amendment 13 - Slavery Abolished. Ratified 12/6/1865.

1. Neither slavery nor involuntary servitude, except as a punishment for crime whereof the party shall have been duly convicted, shall exist within the United States, or any place subject to their jurisdiction.

2. Congress shall have power to enforce this article by appropriate legislation.

Amendment 14 - Citizenship Rights. Ratified 7/9/1868.

1. All persons born or naturalized in the United States, and subject to the jurisdiction thereof, are citizens of the United States and of the State wherein they reside. No State shall make or enforce any law which shall abridge the privileges or immunities of citizens of the United States; nor shall any State deprive any person of life, liberty, or property, without due process of law; nor deny to any person within its jurisdiction the equal protection of the laws.

2. Representatives shall be apportioned among the several States according to their respective numbers, counting the whole number of persons in each State, excluding Indians not taxed. But when the right to vote at any election for the choice of electors for President and Vice-President of the United States, Representatives in Congress, the Executive and Judicial officers of a State, or the members of the Legislature thereof, is denied to any of the male inhabitants of such State, being twenty-one years of age, and citizens of the United States, or in any way abridged, except for participation in rebellion, or other crime, the basis of representation therein shall be reduced in the proportion which the number of such male citizens shall bear to the whole number of male citizens twenty-one years of age in such State.

3. No person shall be a Senator or Representative in Congress, or elector of President and Vice-President, or hold any office, civil or military, under the United States, or under any State, who, having previously taken an oath, as a member of Congress, or as an officer of the United States, or as a member of any State legislature, or as an executive or judicial officer of any State, to support the Constitution of the United States, shall have engaged in insurrection or rebellion against the same, or given aid or comfort to the enemies thereof. But Congress may by a vote of two-thirds of each House, remove such disability.

4. The validity of the public debt of the United States, authorized by law, including debts incurred for payment of pensions and bounties for services in suppressing insurrection or rebellion, shall not be questioned. But neither the United States nor any State shall assume or pay any debt or obligation incurred in aid of insurrection or rebellion against the United States, or any claim for the loss or emancipation of any slave; but all such debts, obligations and claims shall be held illegal and void.

5. The Congress shall have power to enforce, by appropriate legislation, the provisions of this article.

Amendment 15 - Race No Bar to Vote. Ratified 2/3/1870.

1. The right of citizens of the United States to vote shall not be denied or abridged by the United States or by any State on account of race, color, or previous condition of servitude.

2. The Congress shall have power to enforce this article by appropriate legislation.

Amendment 16 - Status of Income Tax Clarified. Ratified 2/3/1913.

The Congress shall have power to lay and collect taxes on incomes, from whatever source derived, without apportionment among the several States, and without regard to any census or enumeration.

Amendment 17 - Senators Elected by Popular Vote. Ratified 4/8/1913.

The Senate of the United States shall be composed of two Senators from each State, elected by the people thereof, for six years; and each Senator shall have one vote. The electors in each State shall have the qualifications requisite for electors of the most numerous branch of the State legislatures.

When vacancies happen in the representation of any State in the Senate, the executive authority of such State shall issue writs of election to fill such vacancies: Provided, That the legislature of any State may empower the executive thereof to make temporary appointments until the people fill the vacancies by election as the legislature may direct.

This amendment shall not be so construed as to affect the election or term of any Senator chosen before it becomes valid as part of the Constitution.

Amendment 18 - Liquor Abolished. Ratified 1/16/1919. Repealed by Amendment 21, 12/5/1933.

1.   After one year from the ratification of this article the manufacture, sale, or transportation of intoxicating liquors within, the importation thereof into, or the exportation thereof from the United States and all territory subject to the jurisdiction thereof for beverage purposes is hereby prohibited.

2.   The Congress and the several States shall have concurrent power to enforce this article by appropriate legislation.

3.   This article shall be inoperative unless it shall have been ratified as an amendment to the Constitution by the legislatures of the several States, as provided in the Constitution, within seven years from the date of the submission hereof to the States by the Congress.

Amendment 19 - Women's Suffrage. Ratified 8/18/1920.

The right of citizens of the United States to vote shall not be denied or abridged by the United States or by any State on account of sex.

Congress shall have power to enforce this article by appropriate legislation.

Amendment 20 - Presidential, Congressional Terms. Ratified 1/23/1933.

1. The terms of the President and Vice President shall end at noon on the 20th day of January, and the terms of Senators and Representatives at noon on the 3d day of January, of the years in which such terms would have ended if this article had not been ratified; and the terms of their successors shall then begin.

2. The Congress shall assemble at least once in every year, and such meeting shall begin at noon on the 3d day of January, unless they shall by law appoint a different day.

3. If, at the time fixed for the beginning of the term of the President, the President elect shall have died, the Vice President elect shall become President. If a President shall not have been chosen before the time fixed for the beginning of his term, or if the President elect shall have failed

to qualify, then the Vice President elect shall act as President until a President shall have qualified; and the Congress may by law provide for the case wherein neither a President elect nor a Vice President elect shall have qualified, declaring who shall then act as President, or the manner in which one who is to act shall be selected, and such person shall act accordingly until a President or Vice President shall have qualified.

4. The Congress may by law provide for the case of the death of any of the persons from whom the House of Representatives may choose a President whenever the right of choice shall have devolved upon them, and for the case of the death of any of the persons from whom the Senate may choose a Vice President whenever the right of choice shall have devolved upon them.

5. Sections 1 and 2 shall take effect on the 15th day of October following the ratification of this article.

6. This article shall be inoperative unless it shall have been ratified as an amendment to the Constitution by the legislatures of three-fourths of the several States within seven years from the date of its submission.

Amendment 21 - Amendment 18 Repealed. Ratified 12/5/1933.

1. The eighteenth article of amendment to the Constitution of the United States is hereby repealed.

2. The transportation or importation into any State, Territory, or possession of the United States for delivery or use therein of intoxicating liquors, in violation of the laws thereof, is hereby prohibited.

3. The article shall be inoperative unless it shall have been ratified as an amendment to the Constitution by conventions in the several States, as provided in the Constitution, within seven years from the date of the submission hereof to the States by the Congress.

Amendment 22 - Presidential Term Limits. Ratified 2/27/1951.

1. No person shall be elected to the office of the President more than twice, and no person who has held the office of President, or acted as President, for more than two years of a term to which some other person was elected President shall be elected to the office of the President more than once. But this Article shall not apply to any person holding the office of President, when this Article was proposed by the Congress, and shall not prevent

any person who may be holding the office of President, or acting as President, during the term within which this Article becomes operative from holding the office of President or acting as President during the remainder of such term.

2.   This article shall be inoperative unless it shall have been ratified as an amendment to the Constitution by the legislatures of three-fourths of the several States within seven years from the date of its submission to the States by the Congress.

Amendment 23 - Presidential Vote for District of Columbia. Ratified 3/29/1961.

1. The District constituting the seat of Government of the United States shall appoint in such manner as the Congress may direct: A number of electors of President and Vice President equal to the whole number of Senators and Representatives in Congress to which the District would be entitled if it were a State, but in no event more than the least populous State; they shall be in addition to those appointed by the States, but they shall be considered, for the purposes of the election of President and Vice President, to be electors appointed by a State; and they shall meet in the District and perform such duties as provided by the twelfth article of amendment.

2.   The Congress shall have power to enforce this article by appropriate legislation.

Amendment 24 - Poll Tax Barred. Ratified 1/23/1964.

1. The right of citizens of the United States to vote in any primary or other election for President or Vice President, for electors for President or Vice President, or for Senator or Representative in Congress, shall not be denied or abridged by the United States or any State by reason of failure to pay any poll tax or other tax.

2. The Congress shall have power to enforce this article by appropriate legislation.

Amendment 25 - Presidential Disability and Succession. Ratified 2/10/1967.

1. In case of the removal of the President from office or of his death or resignation, the Vice President shall become President.

2. Whenever there is a vacancy in the office of the Vice President, the President shall nominate a Vice President who shall take office upon confirmation by a majority vote of both Houses of Congress.

3. Whenever the President transmits to the President pro tempore of the Senate and the Speaker of the House of Representatives his written declaration that he is unable to discharge the powers and duties of his office, and until he

transmits to them a written declaration to the contrary, such powers and duties shall be discharged by the Vice President as Acting President.

4. Whenever the Vice President and a majority of either the principal officers of the executive departments or of such other body as Congress may by law provide, transmit to the President pro tempore of the Senate and the Speaker of the House of Representatives their written declaration that the President is unable to discharge the powers and duties of his office, the Vice President shall immediately assume the powers and duties of the office as Acting President.

Thereafter, when the President transmits to the President pro tempore of the Senate and the Speaker of the House of Representatives his written declaration that no inability exists, he shall resume the powers and duties of his office unless the Vice President and a majority of either the principal officers of the executive department or of such other body as Congress may by law provide, transmit within four days to the President pro tempore of the Senate and the Speaker of the House of Representatives their written declaration that the President is unable to discharge the powers and duties of his office. Thereupon Congress shall decide the issue, assembling within forty eight hours for that purpose if not in session. If the Congress, within twenty one days after receipt of the latter written declaration, or, if

Congress is not in session, within twenty one days after Congress is required to assemble, determines by two thirds vote of both Houses that the President is unable to discharge the powers and duties of his office, the Vice President shall continue to discharge the same as Acting President; otherwise, the President shall resume the powers and duties of his office.

Amendment 26 - Voting Age Set to 18 Years. Ratified 7/1/1971.

1.   The right of citizens of the United States, who are eighteen years of age or older, to vote shall not be denied or abridged by the United States or by any State on account of age.

2.   The Congress shall have power to enforce this article by appropriate legislation.

Amendment 27 - Limiting Congressional Pay Increases. Ratified 5/7/1992.

No law, varying the compensation for the services of the Senators and Representatives, shall take effect, until an election of Representatives shall have intervened.

This file was prepared by and reprinted thanks to USConstitution.net. Find them on the web at http://www.usconstitution.net.

CHARLEY REESE'S FINAL COLUMN

Reprinted from:
www.change.org/p/charley-reese-s-final-column

JUST A FRIENDLY REMINDER

A very interesting column. COMPLETELY NEUTRAL

Be sure to Read the Poem at the end.

Charley Reese's final column for the Orlando Sentinel.

He has been a journalist for 49 years.

He is retiring and this is HIS LAST COLUMN.

Be sure to read the Tax List at the end.

This is about as clear and easy to understand as it can be. The article below is completely neutral, neither anti-republican or democrat. Charlie Reese, a retired reporter for the Orlando Sentinel, has hit the nail directly on the head, defining clearly who it is that in the final analysis must assume responsibility for the judgments made that impact each one of us every day. It's a short but good read. Worth the time. Worth remembering!

545 vs. 300,000,000 People

- By Charlie Reese

Politicians are the only people in the world who create problems and then campaign against them.

Have you ever wondered, if both the Democrats and the Republicans are against deficits, WHY do we have deficits?

Have you ever wondered, if all the politicians are against inflation and high taxes, WHY do we have inflation and high taxes?

You and I don't propose a federal budget. The President does.

You and I don't have the Constitutional authority to vote on appropriations. The House of Representatives does.

You and I don't write the tax code, Congress does.

You and I don't set fiscal policy, Congress does.

You and I don't control monetary policy, the Federal Reserve Bank does.

One hundred senators, 435 congressmen, one President, and nine Supreme Court justices equates to 545 human beings out of the 300 million are directly, legally, morally, and individually responsible for the domestic problems that plague this country.

I excluded the members of the Federal Reserve Board because that problem was created by the Congress. In 1913, Congress delegated its Constitutional duty to provide a sound currency to a federally chartered, but private, central bank.

I excluded all the special interests and lobbyists for a sound reason. They have no legal authority. They have no ability to coerce a senator, a congressman, or a President to do one cotton-picking thing. I don't care if they offer a politician $1 million dollars in cash. The politician has the power to accept or reject it. No matter what the lobbyist promises, it is the legislator's responsibility to determine how he votes.

Those 545 human beings spend much of their energy convincing you that what they did is not their fault. They cooperate in this common con regardless of party.

What separates a politician from a normal human being is an excessive amount of gall. No normal human being would have the gall of a Speaker, who stood up and criticized the President for creating deficits. The President can only propose a budget. He cannot force the Congress to accept it.

The Constitution, which is the supreme law of the land, gives sole responsibility to the House of Representatives for originating and approving appropriations and taxes. Who is the speaker of the House? John Boehner. He is the leader of the majority party. He and fellow House members, not the President, can approve any budget they want. If the President vetoes it, they can pass it over his veto if they agree to.

It seems inconceivable to me that a nation of 300 million cannot replace 545 people who stand convicted -- by present facts -- of incompetence and irresponsibility.. I can't think of a single domestic problem that is not traceable directly to those 545 people. When you fully grasp the plain truth that 545 people exercise the power of the federal government, then it must follow that what exists is what they want to exist.

If the tax code is unfair, it's because they want it unfair.

If the budget is in the red, it's because they want it in the red.

If the Army & Marines are in Iraq and Afghanistan it's because they want them in Iraq and Afghanistan.

If they do not receive social security but are on an elite retirement plan not available to the people, it's because they want it that way.

There are no insoluble government problems.

Do not let these 545 people shift the blame to bureaucrats, whom they hire and whose jobs they can abolish; to lobbyists, whose gifts and advice they can reject; to regulators, to whom they give the power to regulate and from whom they can take this power. Above all, do not let them con you into the belief that there exists disembodied mystical forces like "the economy","inflation," or "politics" that prevent them from doing what they take an oath to do.

Those 545 people, and they alone, are responsible.

They, and they alone, have the power.

They, and they alone, should be held accountable by the people who are their bosses.

Provided the voters have the gumption to manage their own employees.

We should vote all of them out of office and clean up their mess.

Charlie Reese is a former columnist of the Orlando Sentinel Newspaper.

What you do with this article now that you have read it is up to you. This might be funny if it weren't so true. Be sure to read all the way to the end:

Tax his land,

Tax his bed,

Tax the table,

At which he's fed.

Tax his tractor,

Tax his mule,

Teach him taxes

Are the rule.

Tax his work,

Tax his pay,

He works for

peanuts anyway!

Tax his cow,

Tax his goat,

Tax his pants,

Tax his coat.

Tax his ties,

Tax his shirt,

Tax his work,

Tax his dirt.

Tax his tobacco,

Tax his drink,

Tax him if he

Tries to think.

Tax his cigars,

Tax his beers,

If he cries

Tax his tears.

Tax his car,

Tax his gas,

Find other ways

Taxes to pass

Tax all he has

Then let him know

That you won't be done

Till he has no dough.

When he screams and hollers;

Then tax him some more,

Tax him till

He's good and sore.

Then tax his coffin,

Tax his grave,

Tax the sod in

Which he's laid...

Put these words

Upon his tomb,

'Taxes drove me

to my doom...'

When he's gone,

Do not relax,

Its time to apply

The inheritance tax.

Accounts Receivable Tax

Building Permit Tax

CDL license Tax

Cigarette Tax

Corporate Income Tax

Dog License Tax

Excise Taxes

Federal Income Tax

Federal Unemployment Tax (FUTA)

Fishing License Tax

Food License Tax

Fuel Permit Tax

Gasoline Tax (currently 44.75 cents per gallon)

Gross Receipts Tax

Hunting License Tax

Inheritance Tax

Inventory Tax

IRS Interest Charges IRS Penalties (tax on top of tax)

Liquor Tax

Luxury Taxes

Marriage License Tax

Medicare Tax

Personal Property Tax

Property Tax

Real Estate Tax

Service Charge Tax

Social Security Tax

Road Usage Tax

Recreational Vehicle Tax

Sales Tax

School Tax

State Income Tax

State Unemployment Tax (SUTA)

Telephone Federal Excise Tax

Telephone Federal Universal Service Fee Tax

Telephone Federal, State and Local Surcharge Taxes

Telephone Minimum Usage Surcharge Tax

Telephone Recurring and Nonrecurring Charges Tax

Telephone State and Local Tax

Telephone Usage Charge Tax

Utility Taxes

Vehicle License Registration Tax

Vehicle Sales Tax

Watercraft Registration Tax

Well Permit Tax

Workers Compensation Tax

STILL THINK THIS IS FUNNY?

Not one of these taxes existed 100 years ago, and our nation was the most prosperous in the world.

We had absolutely no national debt, had the largest middle class in the world, and Mom stayed home to raise the kids.

What in the heck happened? Can you spell 'politicians?

Reprinted from:
www.change.org/p/charley-reese-s-final-column

The Logic of English®
Level 1
A Compilation of High Frequency Words

1.	rest	35.	hot	69.	as		
2.	me	36.	hat	70.	be		
3.	and	37.	his	71.	sad		
4.	on	38.	if	72.	dog		
5.	at	39.	just	73.	fast		
6.	go	40.	get	74.	sat		
7.	is	41.	men	75.	map		
8.	it	42.	yes	76.	step		
9.	can	43.	ran	77.	fun		
10.	run	44.	ask	78.	flat		
11.	in	45.	lot	79.	sand		
12.	so	46.	soft	80.	cat		
13.	no	47.	sit	81.	bit		
14.	man	48.	send	82.	hit		
15.	top	49.	or	83.	gas		
16.	ten	50.	got	84.	fit		
17.	bed	51.	best	85.	spot		
18.	he	52.	cut	86.	met		
19.	not	53.	yet	87.	gun		
20.	an	54.	spent	88.	wet		
21.	up	55.	sold	89.	jump		
22.	old	56.	plant	90.	bag		
23.	last	57.	most	91.	dust		
24.	us	58.	help	92.	bus		
25.	red	59.	left	93.	bat		
26.	am	60.	glad	94.	rub		
27.	bad	61.	band	95.	slip		
28.	him	62.	set	96.	win		
29.	did	63.	felt	97.	swim		
30.	had	64.	sent	98.	fat		
31.	big	65.	list	99.	dad		
32.	land	66.	stop	100.	log		
33.	hand	67.	held	101.	we		
34.	let	68.	beg				

The Logic of English®
Level 2
A Compilation of High Frequency Words

1.	do	35.	cold	69.	its
2.	a	36.	ice	70.	find
3.	she	37.	street	71.	back
4.	see	38.	child	72.	new
5.	the	39.	late	73.	came
6.	now	40.	ring	74.	take
7.	you	41.	that	75.	went
8.	will	42.	for	76.	give
9.	my	43.	was	77.	show
10.	good	44.	one	78.	form
11.	ago	45.	how	79.	feet
12.	of	46.	them	80.	page
13.	this	47.	then	81.	far
14.	but	48.	some	82.	soon
15.	all	49.	has	83.	told
16.	out	50.	her	84.	thing
17.	into	51.	way	85.	face
18.	like	52.	long	86.	gave
19.	time	53.	day	87.	tree
20.	may	54.	well	88.	add
21.	look	55.	tell	89.	spring
22.	boy	56.	home	90.	free
23.	book	57.	five	91.	ride
24.	six	58.	stand	92.	stone
25.	are	59.	box	93.	song
26.	have	60.	ball	94.	west
27.	by	61.	bring	95.	nine
28.	make	62.	lay	96.	blow
29.	come	63.	led	97.	nice
30.	three	64.	love	98.	dear
31.	must	65.	yard	99.	thank
32.	say	66.	call	100.	end
33.	live	67.	each	101.	lake
34.	play	68.	than	102.	block

The Logic of English®
Level 3
A Compilation of High Frequency Words

1.	little	35.	think	69.	around
2.	your	36.	here	70.	without
3.	today	37.	why	71.	head
4.	over	38.	found	72.	light
5.	school	39.	still	73.	night
6.	mother	40.	air	74.	story
7.	sea	41.	under	75.	better
8.	about	42.	read	76.	across
9.	other	43.	never	77.	city
10.	house	44.	along	78.	upon
11.	door	45.	large	79.	move
12.	eat	46.	blue	80.	open
13.	low	47.	outside	81.	became
14.	baby	48.	boat	82.	become
15.	law	49.	happy	83.	horse
16.	belong	50.	south	84.	class
17.	what	51.	cover	85.	round
18.	very	52.	train	86.	rain
19.	after	53.	east	87.	easy
20.	put	54.	bill	88.	hour
21.	away	55.	report	89.	care
22.	while	56.	sister	90.	glass
23.	paper	57.	forget	91.	clear
24.	letter	58.	noon	92.	week
25.	river	59.	card	93.	maybe
26.	winter	60.	May	94.	reach
27.	miss	61.	palace	95.	party
28.	foot	62.	these	96.	brother
29.	fall	63.	two	97.	wife
30.	north	64.	first	98.	bear
31.	Mr.	65.	only	99.	afternoon
32.	when	66.	water	100.	lady
33.	said	67.	where	101.	hurt
34.	our	68.	any	102.	pound

The Logic of English®
Level 4
A Compilation of High Frequency Words

1. year	35. animals	69. listen
2. Monday	36. problem	70. explain
3. Sunday	37. pour	71. square
4. every	38. window	72. ocean
5. would	39. couldn't	73. climbed
6. could	40. record	74. style
7. should	41. skin	75. money
8. eye	42. wrong	76. brought
9. Friday	43. sign	77. bought
10. July	44. quiet	78. army
11. another	45. scale	79. member
12. however	46. key	80. unable
13. half	47. cotton	81. always
14. war	48. proud	82. young
15. sight	49. poem	83. built
16. pretty	50. plain	84. matter
17. provide	51. rubber	85. history
18. teach	52. potatoes	86. cause
19. study	53. rough	87. wonder
20. wrote	54. council	88. dozen
21. teacher	55. prevent	89. dollar
22. woman	56. watch	90. court
23. subject	57. catch	91. don't
24. rule	58. lead	92. enough
25. prove	59. flower	93. during
26. quite	60. express	94. knew
27. rather	61. suit	95. whole
28. police	62. lesson	96. friend
29. royal	63. news	97. eight
30. does	64. might	98. chief
31. women	65. build	99. station
32. different	66. mountain	100. worth
33. wear	67. leaves	101. address
34. animal	68. main	102. perfect

The Logic of English®
Level 5
A Compilation of High Frequency Words

1.	indeed	35.	regard	69.	purpose
2.	picture	36.	repair	70.	consider
3.	return	37.	vacation	71.	popular
4.	please	38.	important	72.	service
5.	contract	39.	remember	73.	increase
6.	income	40.	special	74.	prepare
7.	inform	41.	measure	75.	success
8.	recover	42.	present	76.	convention
9.	sure	43.	information	77.	illustrate
10.	question	44.	suppose	78.	injure
11.	reason	45.	region	79.	prefer
12.	inspect	46.	result	80.	promise
13.	instead	47.	position	81.	provision
14.	contain	48.	section	82.	publication
15.	public	49.	include	83.	secure
16.	proper	50.	represent	84.	piece
17.	company	51.	president	85.	possible
18.	population	52.	progress	86.	supply
19.	remain	53.	serve	87.	serious
20.	liberty	54.	property	88.	condition
21.	intend	55.	command	89.	improvement
22.	pleasure	56.	connection	90.	investigate
23.	refuse	57.	convict	91.	marriage
24.	request	58.	imprison	92.	mention
25.	restrain	59.	primary	93.	pleasant
26.	retire	60.	private	94.	really
27.	answer	61.	prompt	95.	business
28.	beautiful	62.	publish	96.	various
29.	usual	63.	relative	97.	political
30.	support	64.	complete	98.	concern
31.	reply	65.	common	99.	conference
32.	complaint	66.	machine	100.	impossible
33.	importance	67.	interest	101.	invitation
34.	prison	68.	busy	102.	recent

The Logic of English®
Level 6
A Compilation of High Frequency Words

1. objection	35. discussion	69. groceries
2. according	36. testimony	70. design
3. effect	37. sincerely	71. hospital
4. diamond	38. character	72. bicycle
5. director	39. appreciate	73. soldier
6. distribute	40. athletic	74. structure
7. feature	41. emergency	75. observe
8. honor	42. extreme	76. suggested
9. lose	43. organization	77. dangerous
10. salary	44. especially	78. opportunity
11. treasure	45. disappoint	79. favorite
12. believe	46. decision	80. settled
13. doubt	47. judgement	81. telephone
14. examination	48. distance	82. actually
15. opinion	49. language	83. employee
16. celebration	50. island	84. allowed
17. victim	51. opposite	85. detailed
18. necessary	52. cattle	86. muscles
19. foreign	53. million	87. climate
20. application	54. radio	88. coffee
21. assure	55. similar	89. angle
22. beginning	56. ancient	90. determined
23. circumstance	57. capital	91. dictionary
24. colonies	58. nation	92. ordinary
25. difficulty	59. knowledge	93. arrived
26. distinguish	60. experiment	94. tongue
27. elaborate	61. column	95. activities
28. expense	62. television	96. equipment
29. senate	63. familiar	97. discuss
30. experience	64. oxygen	98. healthy
31. evidence	65. solution	99. frequently
32. arrangement	66. electricity	100. disappear
33. association	67. captain	101. traffic
34. career	68. symbol	102. excited